My full name

_____

Place and date of birth

_____

The person I'm relying on to go through this is (please)

_____

My backup person is (pretty please)

_____

TABLE OF CONTENTS

THE REALLY IMPORTANT STUFF... 7

MY HOME.. 13

MONEY... 19

MY ONLINE LIFE.. 31

REWARDS CARDS.. 41

MY CAREER.. 45

MEDICAL.. 51

ARRANGEMENTS... 55

INSURANCE.. 59

LAWYERS & LEGAL STUFF.. 63

MISCELLANY.. 67

THE REALLY IMPORTANT STUFF

(Yup, it's all about meeeeeee.)

PERSONAL INFO

My phone password, number and provider	
My Social Insurance Number	
My Driver's License Number	
My Passport #	
I am an organ donor	☐ YES ☐ NO

MY FAMILY

My spouse/partner	
My relatives & dependents	

SPECIAL ANIMALS & PEOPLE

My pets, their veterinarian(s) and who has agreed to take them	
My best friends	

NOTES

NOTES

MY HOME
(Sorry if it's a mess.)

MY HOME

My address	
My mortgage # and holder	
My mailbox # and location	
Condo corporation & contact info	
Landlord's name & contact info	
Internet provider & password	
Keyless door password	
Garage door info (fob location, app and/or password)	
Storage locker info	

UTILITIES

Company	Account Number

MY RENTAL PROPERTIES

Address	
Tenant contact info	
Location of lease	

NOTES

NOTES

MONEY
(Cold hard cash...maybe...maybe not.)

MY PRIMARY BANK

Bank transit no.	
Bank institution no.	
Online banking PIN	
Debit card #1 number	
Debit card #1 password	
Debit card PIN	
Debit card #2 number	
Debit card #2 password	
Debit card #2 PIN	
CC #1 number	
CC #1 PIN	
CC #2 number	
CC #2 PIN	
Safe Deposit Box	

ACCOUNT NUMBERS AND TYPE

MY SECONDARY BANK

Bank transit no.	
Bank institution no.	
Online banking PIN	
Debit card #1 number	
Debit card #1 password	
Debit card PIN	
Debit card #2 number	
Debit card #2 password	
Debit card #2 PIN	
CC #1 number	
CC #1 PIN	
CC #2 number	
CC #2 PIN	
Safe Deposit Box	

ACCOUNT NUMBERS AND TYPE

INVESTMENTS

Company & contact	
Company & contact	
Company & contact	

BOOKKEEPING

Company & contact	
Company & contact	
Company & contact	

LOANS, STORE CARDS, ETC.

	Account name
	Password
	Account name
	Password
	Account name
	Password
	Account name
	Password
	Account name
	Password
	Account name
	Password

MONEY TRANSFER ACCOUNTS

	Account name
	Password
	Account name
	Password
	Account name
	Password
	Account name
	Password
	Account name
	Password
	Account name
	Password

NOTES

NOTES

NOTES

MY ONLINE LIFE
(Even the secret stuff...shhhhh...)

SOCIAL MEDIA, WEB SITES & APPS

	Account name
	Password
	Account name
	Password
	Account name
	Password
	Account name
	Password
	Account name
	Password
	Account name
	Password
	Account name
	Password
	Account name
	Password

SOCIAL MEDIA, WEB SITES & APPS

	Account name
	Password
	Account name
	Password
	Account name
	Password
	Account name
	Password
	Account name
	Password
	Account name
	Password
	Account name
	Password
	Account name
	Password

SOCIAL MEDIA, WEB SITES & APPS

	Account name
	Password
	Account name
	Password
	Account name
	Password
	Account name
	Password
	Account name
	Password
	Account name
	Password
	Account name
	Password
	Account name
	Password

SOCIAL MEDIA, WEB SITES & APPS

	Account name
	Password
	Account name
	Password
	Account name
	Password
	Account name
	Password
	Account name
	Password
	Account name
	Password
	Account name
	Password
	Account name
	Password

SOCIAL MEDIA, WEB SITES & APPS

	Account name
	Password
	Account name
	Password
	Account name
	Password
	Account name
	Password
	Account name
	Password
	Account name
	Password
	Account name
	Password
	Account name
	Password

SOCIAL MEDIA, WEB SITES & APPS

	Account name
	Password
	Account name
	Password
	Account name
	Password
	Account name
	Password
	Account name
	Password
	Account name
	Password
	Account name
	Password
	Account name
	Password

MY EMAIL ADDRESSES

Email address	Password
Email address	Password
Email address	Password
Email address	Password
Email address	Password
Email address	Password
Email address	Password
Email address	Password

NOTES

NOTES

REWARDS CARDS
(Don't waste them!)

REWARDS CARDS

	Card #
	Password
	Card #
	Password
	Card #
	Password
	Card #
	Password
	Card #
	Password
	Card #
	Password
	Card #
	Password
	Card #
	Password

NOTES

NOTES

MY CAREER
(Ahhh...no more work.)

WORK INFORMATION

I work for	
My job title	
My boss's name and contact info	
My "side hustle"	

PENSIONS, PAYOUTS & STUFF

NOTES

NOTES

NOTES

MEDICAL
(Hope it's not too complicated.)

MEDICAL INFORMATION

My GP	
My pharmacy	
My health card Number	
My health plan	
My dentist	
Other health care provider	
Other health care provider	
Other health care provider	

NOTES

NOTES

ARRANGEMENTS
(Have a party...or not.)

ARRANGEMENTS

I want my body to go to science. Please contact	
I have made arrangements with	
I have not made pre-arrangments, so would like	☐ A huge party with all of the bells and whistles ☐ Just a quiet interment ☐ A celebration of life located at your discretion a few months down the road
I would also like	☐ To be buried with a headstone ☐ To be cremated and buried with a headstone I would like my headstone to say _____ _____ _____ ☐ To be cremated and put into an urn ☐ To be cremated and scattered here at this location _____

NOTES

NOTES

INSURANCE
(More cash...I hope.)

INSURANCE INFORMATION

My life insurance policy number and contact	
My house insurance policy number and contact	
My car insurance policy number and contact	

NOTES

NOTES

LAWYERS & LEGAL STUFF
(It's all about me...again.)

LAWYERS & LEGAL STUFF

My lawyer is	
My will is located	
My POA is	
My POA is	

NOTES

NOTES

MISCELLANY
(All of the things I couldn't put down anywhere else in this book.)

OTHER STUFF YOU SHOULD KNOW

OTHER STUFF YOU SHOULD KNOW

OTHER STUFF YOU SHOULD KNOW

OTHER STUFF YOU SHOULD KNOW

OTHER STUFF YOU SHOULD KNOW

OTHER STUFF YOU SHOULD KNOW

OTHER STUFF YOU SHOULD KNOW

OTHER STUFF YOU SHOULD KNOW

OTHER STUFF YOU SHOULD KNOW

OTHER STUFF YOU SHOULD KNOW

OTHER STUFF YOU SHOULD KNOW

OTHER STUFF YOU SHOULD KNOW

OTHER STUFF YOU SHOULD KNOW

OTHER STUFF YOU SHOULD KNOW

OTHER STUFF YOU SHOULD KNOW

www.ingramcontent.com/pod-product-compliance
Lightning Source LLC
Chambersburg PA
CBHW081235080526
44587CB00022B/3947